THE KEY OF KNOWLEDGE

THE KEY OF KNOWLEDGE

The Spirit of Truth

Daniel Timothy Bridegroom

To order additional copies of this book, contact:
Xlibris
844-714-8691
www.Xlibris.com
Orders@Xlibris.com
862806

To Know Wisdom and Instruction, to perceive The Words Of Understanding, Proverbs 1:2 To receive The Instruction Of Wisdom, Justice, Judgment, and Equity; 3 To give prudence to the simple, to the young man Knowledge and Discretion---- 4 A wise man will Hear and increase learning, and A Man Of Understanding will attain Wise Counsel. 5

To understand a proverb and an enigma, The Words of the Wise and their riddles. 6 The Fear of The Lord is The Beginning of Knowledge, but fools despise wisdom and instruction. 7 My Son, Hear the Instruction of Your Father, and do not forsake The Law of Your Mother; 8 For they will be a graceful ornament on your head, and chains about your neck. 9

My Son, if sinners entice you, do not consent. 10 If they say, "Come with us, let us lie and wait to shed blood; let us lurk secretly for the innocent without cause; 11 Let us swallow them alive like Sheol, and whole, like those who go down to The Pit; 12 We shall find all kinds of precious possessions, we shall fill our houses with spoil; 13 Cast in your lot among us, let us all have one purse"---- 14

My Son, do not walk in the way with them, keep your foot from their path; 15 For their feet run to evil, and they make haste to shed blood. 16 Surely, in vain the net is spread in the sight of any bird; 17 But they lie in wait for their own blood, they lurk secretly for their own lives. 18

"How long, you simple ones, will you love simplicity? For scorners delight in their scorning, and fools hate Knowledge. 22 Turn at My Rebuke; surely I will pour out My Spirit on you; I will make My Words known to you. 23 Because I called and you refused, I stretched out My Hand and no one regarded. 24 Because you disdained all My Counsel, and would have none of My Rebuke." 25

I also will laugh at your calamity; I will mock when your terror comes, 26 When your terror comes like a storm and your destruction comes like a whirlwind, when distress and anguish come upon you. 27 "Then they will call on Me, but I will not answer; they will seek Me Diligently, but they will not find Me. 28

Because they hated Knowledge, and did not choose The Fear of the Lord, 29 They would have none of My Counsel and despised My every rebuke 30 Therefore they shall eat The Fruit of Their Own Way. And be filled to the full with their own fancies. 31 For the turning away of the simple will slay them, and the complacency of fools will destroy them; 32 But whoever listens to Me will dwell safely, and will be secure, without fear of evil." 33

My Son, if you receive My Words, and treasure My Commands within you, 2:1 So that you incline your ear To Wisdom, and apply your heart To Understanding; 2 Yes, if you cry out For Discernment, and lift up your voice For Understanding, 3 If you seek Her as silver, and Search For Her as for hidden treasure; 4 Then you will Understand The Fear Of The Lord, and find The Knowledge Of God. 5

For The Lord gives Wisdom; From His Mouth Comes Knowledge And Understanding; 6 He stores up Sound Wisdom for The Upright; He Is A Shield to those who Walk Uprightly; 7 He guards The Paths Of Justice, and preserves The Way Of His Saints. 8 Then you will understand Righteousness and Justice, Equity and Every Good Path. 9

When Wisdom enters your heart, and Knowledge is pleasant to your soul, 10 Discretion will preserve you; understanding will keep you, 11 To deliver you from the way of evil, from the man who speaks perverse things, 12 From those who leave The Paths Of Uprightness to walk in the ways of darkness; 13 Who rejoice in doing evil, and delight in the perversity of the wicked; 14 Whose ways are crooked, and who are devious in their paths; 15 To deliver you from the immoral woman, from the seductress who flatters with her words, 16 Who forsakes the companion of her youth, and forgets The Covenant Of Her God. 17

For her house leads down to death and her paths to the dead; 18 None who go to her return, nor do they regain The Paths of Life---- 19 So you may walk in The Way Of Goodness, and keep to The Paths of Righteousness. 20 For the Upright will dwell in the land, and the blameless will remain in it; 21 But the wicked will be cut off from the earth, and the unfaithful will be uprooted from it. 22

My Son, do not forget My Law, but let your heart Keep My Commands; 3:1 For length of days and long life and peace they will add to you, 2 Let not Mercy and Truth forsake you; bind them around your neck, write them on The Tablet Of Your Heart, 3 And so find favor and high esteem in The Sight Of God and man. 4

Trust In the Lord with all your heart, and lean not on your own understanding; 5 In all your ways Acknowledge Him, and He shall direct your paths. 6 Do not be wise in your own eyes; Fear the Lord and depart from evil. 7 It will be health to your flesh, and strength to your bones. 8

My Son, do not despise The Chastening of the Lord, nor detest His Correction; 11 For whom The Lord Loves He corrects, just as a father the son in whom he delights. 12 The Lord by Wisdom founded the earth; By Understanding He established the heavens; 19 By His Knowledge the depths are broken up, and the clouds drop down dew. 20

My Son, let them not depart from your eyes---- Keep Sound Wisdom and Discretion; 21 So they will be life to you soul and grace to your neck. 22 Then you will walk safely in your way, and your foot will not stumble. 23 When you lie down, you will not be afraid; yes, you will lie down and your sleep will be sweet. 24

My Son, give attention to My Words; incline you ear to My Sayings, 4:20 Do not let them depart from your eyes; keep them in the midst of your heart; 21 For they are life to those who find them, and health to all their flesh, 22 Keep your heart with all diligence, for out of it spring The Issues Of Life. 23

My Son, pay attention to My Wisdom; lend your ear to My Understanding, 5:1 That you may preserve discretion, and your lips may keep Knowledge. 2 For the ways of man are before The Eyes of the Lord, and He ponders all his paths. 21 His own iniquities entrap the wicked man, and he is caught in the cords of his sin. 22

These six things The Lord hates, yes, seven are an abomination to Him: 6:16 A proud look, a lying tongue, hands that shed innocent blood, 17 A heart that devises wicked plans, feet that are swift in running to evil, 18 A false witness who speaks lies, and one who sows discord among brethren. 19

"To you, O men, I Call, and My Voice is to the sons of men, 8:4 O you simple ones, understand prudence, and you fools, be of an understanding heart. 5 Listen, for I will speak of excellent things, and from the opening of My Lips will come Right Things; 6 For My Mouth Will Speak Truth; wickedness is an abomination to My Lips. 7 All the Words of My Mouth are with Righteousness; nothing crooked or perverse is in them. 8 They are all plain to him who understands and Right to those who Find Knowledge." 9

"The Fear of the Lord is The Beginning of Wisdom, and The Knowledge of the Holy One is Understanding.

9:10 For By Me you days will be multiplied, and years of Life will be added to you. 11 If you are wise, you are wise for yourself, and if you scoff, you will bear it alone." 12

The Fear of the Lord prolongs days, but the years of the wicked will be shortened. 10:27 The Hope of The Righteous will be gladness, but the expectation of the wicked will perish. 28 The Way of The Lord is Strength for The Upright, but destruction will come to the workers of iniquity. 29

When pride comes, then comes shame; but with the humble is wisdom. 11:2 The Integrity of The Upright will guide them, but the perversity of the unfaithful will destroy them. 3 The Righteousness of the blameless will direct his way aright, but the wicked will fall by his own wickedness. 5

The hypocrite with his mouth destroys his neighbor, but through Knowledge the Righteous will be delivered. 9 When it goes well with The Righteous, the city rejoices; and when the wicked perish, there is jubilation. 10 As Righteousness leads to Life, so he who pursues evil pursues it to his own death. 19

He who despises The Word will be destroyed, but he who Fears the Commandment will be rewarded. 13:13 The Law Of The Wise is A Fountain of Life, to turn one away from the snares of death. 14 Every prudent man Acts With Knowledge, but a fool lays open his folly. 16

O God, You Are My God; Early will I Seek You; My Soul Thirsts for You; My Flesh Longs for You in a dry and thirsty land where there is no water. Psalms 63:1

So I Have Looked For You in the Sanctuary, To See Your Power and Your Glory. 2 Because Your Lovingkindness Is Better Than Life, My Lips shall Praise You. 3

Thus, I Will Bless You while I Live; I Will Lift Up My Hands IN YOUR NAME. 4 My soul shall be satisfied as with marrow and fatness, and My Mouth Shall Praise You with Joyful Lips. 5 When I Remember You on My bed, I Meditate on You in The Night Watches. 6 Because You Have Been My Help, therefore In The Shadow Of Your Wings I Will Rejoice. 7

My soul follows close behind You, Your Right Hand Upholds Me. 8 But those who seek My Life, to destroy it, shall go into the lower parts of the earth. 9 They shall fall by The Sword; they shall be portion for jackals. 10 But the King Shall Rejoice IN GOD; everyone who swears By Him shall Glory, but the mouth of those who speak lies shall be stopped. 11

As they departed, Jesus began to say to the multitudes concerning John: "What did you go out into the wilderness to see? A reed shaken by the wind? Matthew 11:7 But what did you go out to see? A man clothed in soft garments? Indeed those who wear soft garments are in kings' houses. 8 But what did you go out to see? A Prophet? Yes. I say to you, and more than A Prophet." 9

"For this is He of whom it is written: 'Behold, I Send My Messenger before your face, who will prepare Your Way before you.' 10 Assuredly, I say to you, among those born of women there has not One Risen greater than John the Baptist; But 'He Who Is Least in the Kingdom of Heaven Is Greater Than He.' 11 And if you are willing To Receive It, He Is Elijah Who Is To Come. 14 He who hath ears to hear let him hear!" 15

"But to what shall I liken this generation? It is like children sitting in the marketplaces and calling to their companions, 16 And saying: 'We played the flute for You, and You did not dance; we mourned to You, and You did not lament.'" 17

"For John came neither eating nor drinking, and they say, 'He has a demon.' 18 The Son of Man came eating and drinking, and they say, 'Look, a glutton and a winebibber, a friend of tax collectors and sinners!' But Wisdom is justified by her children. 19 Then He began to rebuke the cities in which most of His Mighty Works had been done, because they did not repent: 20 'But I say to you that it shall be more tolerable for the land of Sodom in The Day Of Judgment than for you.'" 24

"Behold! My Servant whom I Have Chosen, My Beloved in whom My Soul is well pleased! I Will Put MY SPIRIT upon Him, and He Will Declare Justice To The Gentiles. 12:18 He will not quarrel nor cry out, nor will anyone hear His Voice in the streets. 19 A bruised reed He will not break, and smoking flax He will not quench, till He Sends Forth Justice to Victory; 20 And IN HIS NAME Gentiles will trust." 21

"Brood of vipers! How can you being evil, speak good things? For out pf the abundance of the heart the mouth speaks. 34 A good man out of the good treasure of his heart brings forth good things, and an evil man out of the evil treasure brings forth evil things. 35 But I say to you that for every idle word men may speak, they will give account of it In the Day of Judgment. 36 For by your words you will be justified, and by your words you will be condemned." 37

Do not fret of evildoers, nor be envious of the workers of iniquity. Psalms 37:1 For they shall soon be cut down like the grass, and wither like the green herb. 2 Trust in The Lord, and do good; dwell in the land, and feed on His Faithfulness. 3 Delight yourself also in The Lord, and He shall give you the desires of your heart. 4

Commit your way to The Lord, trust also in Him, and He shall bring it to pass. 5 He shall bring forth your righteousness as the light, and your justice as the noonday. 6 Rest in The Lord, and wait patiently for Him; do not fret because of him who prospers in his way, because of the man who brings wicked schemes to pass. 7 Cease from anger, and forsake wrath; do not fret---- it only causes harm. 8

For evildoers shall be cut off; but those who wait on The Lord, they shall inherit the earth. 9 For yet a little while and the wicked shall be no more; indeed, you will look carefully for his place, but it shall be no more. 10 But the meek shall inherit the earth, and shall delight themselves in The Abundance of Peace. 11

The wicked plots against The Just, and gnashes at him with his teeth. 12 The Lord laughs at him, for He Sees that his day is coming. 13 The wicked have drawn the sword and have bent their bow, to cast down the poor and needy, to slay those who are of Upright

Conduct. 14 Their sword shall enter their own heart, and their bows shall be broken. 15

A little that A Righteous Man has is better than the riches of many wicked. 16 For the arm of the wicked shall be broken, but The Lord Upholds the Righteous. 17 The Lord knows The Days of the Upright, and their inheritance shall be forever. 18 They shall not be ashamed in the evil time, and in the days of famine, they shall be satisfied. 19

But the wicked shall perish; and the enemies of The Lord, like the splendor of the meadows, shall vanish. Into smoke, they shall vanish. 20 The wicked borrows and does not repay, but the righteous shows mercy and gives. 21 For those Blessed by Him shall inherit the earth, but those cursed By Him shall be cut off. 22

The Steps of a Good Man are Ordered by the Lord, and He Delight in His Way. 23 Though he fall, he shall not be utterly cast down; for The Lord upholds him with His Hand. 24 I have been young, and now AM old; yet I have not seen the righteous forsaken, nor his descendants begging bread. 25 He is ever merciful, and lends; and his descendants are blessed. 26

Depart from evil, and do good; and dwell forevermore. 27 For the Lord loves Justice, and does not forsake His Saints; they are preserved forever, but the descendants of the wicked shall be cut off. 28 The Righteous shall inherit the land, and dwell in it forever. 29

The Mouth Of The Righteous Speaks Wisdom, and His Tongue Talks Of Justice. 30 The Law of His God is in His Heart; none of His Steps shall slide. 31 The wicked watches the righteous, and seek to slay Him. 32 The Lord will not leave Him in his hand, nor condemn Him when He is judged. 33

Wait on The Lord, and Keep His Way, and He shall exalt you to inherit the land; when the wicked are cut off, you shall see it. 34 I have seen the wicked in great power, and spreading himself like a native green tree. 35 Yet he pass away, and Behold, he was no more; indeed, I sought him, but he could not be found. 36

Mark the blameless man, and observe The Upright; for The Future of That Man Is Peace. 37 But the transgressors shall be destroyed together; the future of the wicked shall be cut off. 38 But the Salvation of the Righteous is from The Lord; He is their strength in The Time of Trouble. 39 And the Lord shall help them and deliver them; He shall deliver them from the wicked, and save them, because they Trust In Him. 40

He Sent Them to Preach the Kingdom of God and to heal the sick. Luke 9:2 And He said to them, "Take nothing for The Journey, neither staff nor bag nor bread nor money; and do not have two tunics apiece. 3 Whatever house you enter, stay there, and from there depart. 4 And whoever will not receive you. When you go out of that city, shake off the very dust from your feet as a testimony against them." 5

And it happened as He was alone praying that His Disciples joined Him, and He asked them, saying, "Who do the crowds say that I AM?" 18 So they answered and said, "John the Baptist, but some say Elijah; and other say that one of The Old Prophets has risen again." 19

He said to them, "But who do you say that I AM?" Peter answered and said, "THE CHRIST OF GOD." 20 And He strictly warned and commanded them to tell this to know one, 21 Saying, "The Son Of Man must suffer many things, and Be Rejected by the elders and chief priests and scribes, and be killed, and be raised The Third Day." 22

Then He said to them all, "If anyone desires To Come After Me, let him deny himself, and take up his cross daily, and Follow Me. 23 For whoever desires to save his life will lose it, but whoever loses his life For My Sake will save it. 24

For what profit is it to a man if he gains the whole world, and is himself destroyed or lost?" 25

"For whoever is ashamed of Me and My Words, of him The Son Of Man will be ashamed when He Comes In His Own Glory, and In His Father's, and of The Holy Angels. 26 But I tell you truly, there are some standing here who shall not taste death till they see the Kingdom of God." 27

O God, why have You cast us off forever? Why does Your Anger smoke against The Sheep of Your Pasture? Psalms 74:1 Remember Your Congregation, which You Have Purchased of Old, The Tribe Of Your Inheritance, which You Have Redeemed---- This Mount Zion where You Have Dwelt. 2

Lift up Your Feet to The Perpetual Desolations. The enemy has damaged everything in The Sanctuary. 3 Your enemies roar in the midst of Your Meeting Place;

they set up their banners for signs. 4 They seem like men who lift up axes among the thick trees. 5

And now they break down its carved works, all at once, with axes and hammers. 6 They have set fire to Your Sanctuary; they have defiled The Dwelling Place of Your Name to the ground. 7 They said in their hearts, "Let us destroy them altogether. "They have burned up all The Meeting Places of God in the land." 8

We do not see our signs; there is no longer any prophets; nor is there any who knows how long. O God, how long will the adversary reproach? Will the enemy blaspheme Your Name forever? 10 Why do You withdraw Your Hand, even Your Right Hand? Take it out of Your bosom and destroy them. 11

For God is My King from of old, Working Salvation in the midst of the earth. 12 You divided the sea by Your Strength; You broke the heads of the sea serpents in the waters. 13 You broke the heads of Leviathan in pieces, and gave him as food to the people inhabiting the wilderness. 14 You broke open the fountain and the flood; You dried up mighty rivers. 15 The Day Is Yours, the night also Is Yours; You have prepared The Light and The Sun. 16 You have set all the borders of the earth; you made summer and winter. 17

Remember This, that the enemy has reproached, O Lord, and that a foolish people has blasphemed Your Name. 18 Oh, do not deliver the life of Your turtledove to the wild beast! Do not forget the life of Your poor forever. 19 Have respect To the Covenant; for the dark places of the earth are full of the haunts of cruelty. 20

Oh, do not let the oppressed Return ashamed! Let the poor and needy Praise Your Name. 21 ARISE, O GOD, plead Your Own Cause; remember how the foolish man reproaches You daily. 22 Do not forget the voice of Your enemies; the tumult of those who rise up against You increases continually. 23

But although He had done so many signs before them, they did not Believe in Him, John 12:37 That the word of Isaiah the Prophet might be fulfilled, which he spoke: "Lord, who has Believed Our Report? And To whom has The Arm of The Lord been Revealed?" 38

Therefore they could not Believe, because Isaiah said again: 39 "He has blinded their eyes and hardened their hearts, lest they should see with their eyes, lest they should understand with their hearts and TURN, so that I should heal them." 40 These things Isaiah said when He Saw His Glory and Spoke of Him. 41

Nevertheless even among the rulers many Believed In Him, but because of the Pharisees they did not confess Him, lest they should be put out of The Synagogue; 42 for they loved the praise of men more than The Praise of God. 43 Then Jesus cried out and said, "He who Believes In Me, believes not In Me 'But in Him Who Sent Me'. 44 And he who See Me Sees Him who Sent Me," 45

"For I have not spoken on My own authority; but The Father who Sent Me gave Me a Command, what I should say and what I should speak. 49 And I know that His Command Is Everlasting Life. Therefore, whatever I speak, just as The Father has told Me, so I speak." 50

"Let not your heart be troubled; you Believe In God, Believe also In Me. 14:1 In My Father's House are many mansions; if it were not so, I would have told you. I go to prepare A Place for you. 2 And if I go and prepare A Place for you, I Will Come Again and Receive you To Myself; that where I AM, there you may be also. 3 And where I Go you know, and The Way you know." 4

Jesus said to him, "I AM The Way, The Truth, and The Life. No one comes to The Father except through Me. 6 If you had known Me, you would have known My Father also; and from now on you know Him and Have seen Him. 7 Do you not Believe that I AM In the Father, and The Father In Me? The Words that I speak to you I do not speak on My own authority; but The Father Who Dwells In Me Does the Works." 10

"He who hates Me hates My Father also. 15:23 If I had not done among them The Works which no one else did, they would have no sin; but now they have seen and also hated both Me and My Father. 24 But this happened that The Word might be fulfilled which is written in their law, 'They hated Me without a cause.' 25 But when the Helper Comes, whom I Shall Send to you From the Father, The Spirit of Truth who proceeds From the Father, He will Testify of Me." 26

"These Things I have spoken to you that you should not be made to stumble. 16:1 They will put you out of the synagogues; yes, the time is coming that whoever kills you will think that he offers God service. 2 And these things they will do to you because they have not known The Father nor Me." 3

"Nevertheless I tell you The Truth. It is to you advantage that I go away; for if I do not go away, The Helper will not come to you; but if I depart, I will Send Him to you. 7 And when He Comes, He will convict the world of sin, and of righteousness, and of Judgment: 8 Of sin, because they do not Believe In Me; 9 Of righteousness, because I go to My Father and you see Me no more; 10 Of judgment, because the ruler of this world is judged." 11

"However, when He, The Spirit of Truth, Has Come, He will guide you Into All Truth; He will not speak on His own authority, but whatever He Hears He will speak; and He Will Tell You Things to Come. 13 He Will Glorify Me, for He will take of what is Mine and Declare it to you." 14

All inhabitants of the world and dwellers on the earth: when He lifts up A Banner on the mountains, you see it; and when He blows A Trumpet, you hear it. Isaiah 18:3 For the Lord said to Me, "I will take My Rest, and I will look from My Dwelling Place like clear heat in sunshine, like a cloud of dew in the heat of harvest." 4

For before The Harvest, when the bud is perfect and the souring grape is ripening in the flower, He will both cut off the sprigs with pruning hooks and take away and cut down the branches. 5 They will be left together for the mountain birds of prey and for the beasts of the earth; the bird of prey will summer on them, and all the beasts of the earth will winter on them. 6

In That Time a present will be brought to The Lord of Hosts from a people tall and smooth of skin and from a people terrible from their beginning onward, a nation powerful and treading down, whose land the rivers divide---- to The Place Of The Name Of The Lord Of Hosts, To Mount Zion. 7

For The Lord will comfort Zion, He will comfort all her waste places; He will make Her wilderness Like Eden, and Her desert Like The Garden Of The Lord; Joy and Gladness will be found in It, Thanksgiving and The Voice Of Melody. 51:3 Listen to Me, My People; and give ear to Me, O My Nation: For Law will proceed From Me, and I will make My Justice rest as a light of the peoples. 4

My Righteousness Is Near, My Salvation has gone forth, and My Arms will judge the peoples; the coastlands will wait upon Me, and On My Arm they will trust. 5 Lift up your eyes to the heavens, and look to the earth beneath. For the heavens will vanish away like smoke, the earth will grow old like a garment, and those who dwell in it will die in like manner, But My Salvation will be Forever, and My Righteousness will not be abolished. 6

So The Ransomed of the Lord shall Return, and Come to Zion with singing, with Everlasting Joy on their heads. They shall obtain Joy and Gladness; sorrow and sighing shall flee away. 11 And I have put My Words in your mouth; I have covered you with The Shadow of My Hand that I may plant the heavens, lay the foundations of the earth, and say To Zion, "You are My People". 16

We have heard with our ears, O God, our fathers have told us, The Deeds You Did in their days, in days of old. Psalms 44:1 You drove out the nations with Your Hand, but then you planted; you afflicted the peoples, and cast them out. 2 For they did not gain possession of the land by their own sword, nor did their own arm save them; but it was Your Right Hand, Your Arm, and The Light Of Your Countenance, because You Favored Them. 3

You are My King, O God; command victories for Jacob. 4 Through You we will push down our enemies; through Your Name we will trample those who rise up against us. 5 For I will not trust in My bow, nor shall My sword save Me. 6 But You have Saved Us from our enemies, and have put to shame those who hated us. 7 In God we boast all day long, and Praise Your Name Forever. Selah (Chosen Future) 8

But You have cast us off and put us to shame, and You do not go out with our armies. 9 You make us turn back from the enemy, and those who hate us have taken spoil for themselves. 10 You have given us up as if sheep intended for food, and have scattered us among the nations. 11

You sell Your people for next to nothing, and are not enriched by selling them. 12 You make us a reproach to our neighbors, a scorn and a derision to those all around us. 13 You make us a byword among the nations, a shaking of the head among the peoples. 14

My dishonor is continually before Me, and shame on My Face has covered Me, 15 Because of the voice of him who reproaches and reviles, because of the enemy and the avenger, 16 All this has come upon us; but we have not forgotten You, nor have we dealt falsely with Your Covenant. 17

Our heart has not turned back, nor have our steps departed from Your Way; 18 But You have severely broken us in the place of jackals, and covered us with The Shadow of Death. 19 If we had forgotten The Name of Our God, or stretched out our hand to a foreign god, 20 Would God not search this out? For He Knows the secrets of the heart. 21

Yet for Your Sake we are killed all day long; we are accounted as sheep for the slaughter. 22 Awake! Why do You sleep, O Lord? Arise! Do not cast us off forever. 23 Why do you hide Your Face, and forget our affliction and our oppression? For our soul is bowed down to the dust; our body clings to the ground. 25 Arise for Our Help, and Redeem Us For Your Mercies' Sake. 26

"Son of Man, set Your Face toward Jerusalem, preach against the holy places, and prophesy against the land of Israel; Ezekiel 21:2 And say to the land of Israel, 'Thus says The Lord: "Behold, I AM against you, and I will draw My Sword out of its sheath and cut off both righteous and wicked from you. 3 Because I will cut off both righteous and wicked from you, therefore My Sword shall go out of its sheath against all flesh from south to north, 4 That all flesh may know that I, The Lord, have drawn My Sword out of its sheath; it shall not return anymore."'" 5

"Sigh therefore, Son of Man, with a breaking heart, and sigh with bitterness before their eyes. 6 And it shall be when they say to You, 'Why are you sighing?' that

You shall answer, 'Because of the news; when it comes, every heart will melt, all hands will be feeble, every spirit will faint, and all knees will be weak as water. Behold it is coming and shall be brought to pass,' says The Lord God." 7

Overthrown, Overthrown, I will make it Overthrown! It shall be no longer, until HE COMES WHOSE RIGHT IT IS, AND I WILL GIVE IT TO HIM. 27 The nations shall see and be ashamed of all their might; they shall put their hand over their mouth; their ears shall be deaf. Micah 7:16 They shall lick the dust like a serpent; they shall crawl from their holes like snakes of the earth. They shall be afraid of The Lord Our God, and shall fear because of You. 17

Who is A God like You, pardoning iniquity and passing over the transgression of The Remnant of His Heritage? He does not retain His Anger forever, because He Delights in Mercy. 18 He will again have compassion on us, and will subdue our iniquities. You will cast all our sins into the depths of the sea. 19 You will give Birth to Jacob and Mercy to Abraham. Which You Have Sworn to Fathers from days of old. 20

The Mountains Quake before Him, the hills melt, and the earth heaves At His Presence, yes, The World and all who dwell in it. Nahum 1:5 Who can stand before His Indignation? And who can endure The Fierceness of His Anger? His Fury is poured out like fire, and the rocks are thrown down by Him. 6 What do you conspire against The Lord? He will make an utter end of it. Affliction will not rise up a second time. 8

The Lord has given A Command concerning you: "Your name shall be perpetuated no longer. Out of the house of your gods, I will cut off the carved images and the molded images. I will dig your grave, for you are vile." 14 Behold, on the mountains the feet of Him who brings Good Tidings, who Proclaims Peace! O Judah, keep your appointed feasts, perform your vows. For the wicked one shall no more pass through you; he is utterly cut off. 15

Does not Wisdom cry out, and understanding lift up her voice? Proverbs 8:1 She take her stand on the top of the high hill, beside The Way, where the paths meet. 2 She cries out be the gates, at the entry of the city, at the entrance of the doors: 3 "To you, O men, I call, and my voice is to the sons of men. 4 O you simple ones, understand prudence, and you fools, be of an understanding heart." 5

"Listen, for I will speak of excellent things, and from the opening of My Lips will come Right Things; 6 For My Mouth will speak truth; wickedness is an abomination to My Lips. 7 All the Words of My Mouth are with Righteousness; nothing crooked or perverse is in them 8 They are all plain to Him who understands, and Right to those who find knowledge. 9

SAMEK: I hate the double-minded, but I Love Your Law. Psalms 119:113 You are My Hiding Place and My Shield; I Hope in Your Word. 114 Depart from Me, you evildoers, for I will keep The Commandments Of My God! 115 Uphold Me according to Your Word, that I May Live; and do not let Me be ashamed of My Hope. 116

Hold Me up. And I shall be safe, and I shall observe Your Statutes continually, 117 You reject all those who stray from Your Statutes, for their deceit is falsehood. 118 You put away all the wicked of the earth like dross; therefore I Love Your Testimonies. 119 My flesh trembles for Fear Of You, and I AM afraid of Your Judgments. 120

AYIN: I have done Justice and Righteousness; do not leave Me to My oppressors. 121 Be Surety for Your Servant for Good; do not let the proud oppress Me. 122 My eyes fail from Seeking Your Salvation and Your Righteous Word. 123 Deal with Your Servant according to Your Mercy, and Teach Me Your Statutes. 124

I AM Your Servant; give Me Understanding, that I may know Your Testimonies. 125 It Is Time For Your To Act, O Lord, for they have regarded Your Law as void. 126 Therefore I Love Your Commandments more than gold, yes, than fine gold! 127 Therefore all Your Precepts concerning All Things I consider to be Right; I hate every false way. 128

And The Lord said to the woman, "What is this that you have done?" The woman said, "The serpent deceived me, and I ate." Genesis 3:13 So the Lord God said to the serpent: "Because you have done this, you are cursed more than all cattle, and more than every beast of the field; on you belly you shall go and you shall eat dust all the days of your life. 14 And I will put enmity between you and the woman, and between your seed and her seed; He shall bruise your head and you shall bruise his heel." 15

Then The Lord God said, "Behold, the man has become like one of Us, to know Good and evil. And Now, lest he put out of his hand and take also of The Tree of Life, and eat, and live forever"---- 2 So He drove out the man; and He placed cherubim at the east of The Garden of Eden, and A Flaming Sword which turned every way, to guard The Way to The Tree of Life. 24

And He showed me A Pure River of Water Of Life, clear as crystal, proceeding from The Throne of God and Of the Lamb. Revelation 22:1 In the middle of its street, and on either side of The River, was The Tree Of Life, which bore twelve fruits, each tree yielding its fruit every month. The Leaves of The Tree were for The Healing of the Nations. 2 And there shall be no more curse, but The Throne of God and Of the Lamb shall be in It, and His Servants Shall Serve Him. 3

When The Lord brought back The Captivity of Zion, we were like those who dream. Psalms 126:1 Then our mouth was filled with laughter, and our tongue with singing. Then they said among the nations, "The Lord Has Done Great Things for Them." 2 The Lord has done great things for Us, and We Are Glad. 3

Bring back our captivity, O Lord, as the streams in the south. 4 Those who Sow In Tears Shall Reap In Joy. 5 He who continually goes forth weeping, bearing seed for sowing, shall doubtless come again with Rejoicing, bringing his sheaves with him. 6

Lord, Remember David and all his afflictions; Psalms 132:1 How He swore to The Lord, and vowed to The Mighty One of Jacob: 2 "Surely I will not go into the chamber of my house, or go up to the comfort of my bed; 3 I will not give sleep to my eyes or slumber to my eyelids, 4 Until I find A Place for The Lord, A Dwelling Place For The Mighty One Of Jacob." 5

Behold, we heard of It in Ephrathah; we found it in The Fields of the Woods. 6 Let us go into His Tabernacle; let us Worship at His Footstool. 7 Arise, O Lord, to Your Resting Place, You and The Ark Of Your Strength. 8 Let Your priests be clothed with Righteousness, and let Your Saints Shout for Joy. 9

For Your Servant David's Sake, do not turn away The Face of Your Anointed. 10 The Lord has sworn In Truth to David; He will not turn from it: "I will set upon Your Throne the fruit of your body. 11 If your sons will Keep My Covenant and My Testimony which I shall teach them, their sons also shall sit upon Your Throne Forevermore." 12

For The Lord Has Chosen Zion; He has desired it for His Dwelling Place: 13 "This is My Resting Place forever; here I will dwell, for I have desired it. 14 I will abundantly bless her provision; I will satisfy her poor with bread. 15 I will also clothe her priests with Salvation, and her saints shall shout aloud for joy. 16 There I will make The Horn of David grow; I will prepare A Lamp for My Anointed. 17 His enemies I will clothe with shame, but upon Himself His Crown shall flourish." 18

"Who is this who darkens counsel by words without knowledge? Job 38:2 Now prepare yourself like a man; I will question you, and you shall answer Me. 3 Where were you when I laid The Foundations of the earth? Tell

Me, if you have understanding. 4 Who determined its measurements? Surely you know! Or who stretched the line upon it?" 5

To what were its foundations fastened? Or who laid its Cornerstone, 6 When the Morning Stars sang together, and all The Sons of God shouted for joy? 7 "Or who shut in the sea with doors, when it burst forth and issued from the womb; 8 When I made the clouds its garment, and thick darkness its swaddling band; 9 When I fixed My Limit for it, and set bars and doors; 10 When I said, 'This far you may come, but no farther, and here your proud waves must stop!'" 11

"Have you command the morning since your days began, and caused the dawn to know its place, 12 That it might take hold of The Ends Of The Earth, and the wicked be shaken out of it? 13 It takes on form like clay under a seal, and stands out like a garment. 14 From the wicked their light is withheld, and the upraised arm is broken. 15

"Have you entered the springs of the sea? Or have you walked in search of the depths? 16 Have the gates of death been revealed to you? Or have you seen The Doors of the Shadow of Death? 17 Have you comprehended The Breath of the earth? Tell Me, if you know all this." 18

Then Job answered The Lord and said: Job 42:1 "I know that You can do everything, and that no purpose of Yours can be withheld from You. 2 You asked, 'Who is this who hides counsel without knowledge? Therefore I have uttered what I did not understand, things too wonderful for me, which I did not know.' 3 Listen,

Please, and let me speak; You said, 'I will question you, and you shall answer Me.' 4 I have heard of You by the hearing of the ear, but now my eye sees You.'" 5

"Hear The Word Of The Lord, O nations, and declare it in the isles afar off, and say, He who scattered Israel will gather him, and keep him As A Shepherd does His Flock. Jeremiah 31:10 For the Lord Hath Redeemed Jacob, and Ransomed Him from the hand of one stronger than him. 11 Therefore they shall Come and Sing in The Height Of Zion, streaming to The Goodness Of The Lord---- for wheat and new wine and oil, for the young of the flock and the herd; their souls shall be like a well-watered garden, and they shall sorrow no more at all." 12

Thus says The Lord of Hosts, The God of Israel: "They shall again use This Speech in The Land of Judah and in its cities, when I bring back their captivity: 'The Lord Bless You, O Home of Justice, And Mountain of Holiness!' 23 And there shall dwell in Judah itself, and in all its cities together, Farmers and those going out with flocks. 24 For I have satiated the weary soul, and I have replenished every sorrowful soul." 26

"Behold, The Days Are Coming, says The Lord, when I will make A New Covenant with The House Of Israel and with The House Of Judah---- 31 Not according to The Covenant that I made with their fathers in the day that I took them by The Hand to bring them out of the land of Egypt, My Covenant which they broke, though I was a husband to them, says The Lord." 32

"But this is The Covenant that I will make with The House of Israel after Those Days, says The Lord: 'I will put My Law in their minds and Write It on their hearts; and I will Be Their God, and they shall Be My People. 33 No More shall every man teach his neighbor, and every man his brother, saying, 'Know The Lord,' for They All Shall Know Me, from the least of them to the greatest of them, says The Lord. For I will forgive their iniquity, and their sin I will remember no more." 34

"Behold, the Days Are Coming, says The Lord, that The City Shall Be Built for the Lord from The Tower Of Hananel to The Corner Gate. 38 The surveyor's line shall again extend straight forward over The Hill Gareb; then it shall turn toward Goath.39 And the whole valley of the dead bodies and of the ashes, and all the fields as far as The Brook Kidron, to The Corner Of The Horse Gate toward the east, Shall Be Holy To The Lord. It shall not be plucked up or thrown down Anymore Forever." 40

"Thus says The Lord who made it, The Lord who formed it to establish it (The Lord Is His Name): 33:1 'Call to Me, and I will answer you, and show you great and mighty things, which you do not know.' 3 'Behold, I will bring it health and healing; I will heal them and Reveal to them The Abundance of Peace and Truth.'" 6

"And I will cause The Captives of Judah and The Captives of Israel to Return, and will build those places as at the First. 7 I will cleanse them from all their iniquity by which they have sinned against Me, and I will pardon all their iniquities by which they have sinned and by which they have transgressed against Me. 8 Then it shall be to Me A Name, A Praise, and An Honor before all the nations of the earth, who shall hear all The Good that I do to them; they shall fear and tremble for all The Goodness and all The Prosperity that I provide for It." 9

"Thus says The Lord: 'Again there shall be heard in this place---- of which you say, "It is desolate, without man and without beast"---- in the cities of Judah, in The Streets Of Jerusalem that are desolate, without man and without inhabitant and without beast. 10 The Voice Of Joy and The Voice Of Gladness, The Voice Of The Bridegroom and The Voice Of The Bride, The Voice of those who will say: "Praise The Lord Of Hosts. For The Lord Is Good, for His Mercies Endure Forever"---- and of those who will bring The Sacrifice of Praise into The House of the Lord. For I will cause the captives of the land To Return as at the First,'" Says the Lord. 11

I will love You, O Lord, My Strength. Psalms 18:1 The Lord is My Rock and My Fortress and My Deliver; My God, My Strength, My Strength, in whom I will trust; My Shield and The Horn Of My Salvation, My Stronghold. 2 I will call upon The Lord, who is worthy to be praised; so shall I be saved from my enemies. 3

The pangs of death surrounded me, and the floods of ungodliness made me afraid. 4 The sorrows of Sheol surrounded me; the snares of death confronted me. 5 In my distress I called upon The Lord, and cried out to My God; He heard My Voice from His Temple, and my cry came before Him; even to His Ears. 6

Then the earth shook and trembled; the foundations of the hills also quaked and were shaken, because He was angry. 7 Smoke went up from His Nostrils, and devouring fire From His Mouth; coals were kindled by it. 8 He bowed the heavens also, and came down with darkness under His Feet. 9 And He rode upon A Cherub, and flew; He flew upon the wings of the wind. 10

He made darkness His Secret Place; His Canopy around Him was dark waters and thick clouds of the skies. 11 From the brightness before Him, His thick clouds passed with hailstones and coals of fire. 12 The Lord thundered from heaven, and The Most High uttered His Voice, hailstones and coals of fire. 13

He sent out His Arrows and scattered the foe, lightning is in abundance, and He vanquished them. 14 Then the Channels OF The Sea were seen, the foundations of the world were uncovered at Your Rebuke, O Lord, at The Blast of the Breath of Your Nostrils. 15 He sent from above, He took Me; He drew Me out of many waters. 16

He Delivered Me from my strong enemy, from those who hated Me, for they were too strong for Me. 17 They confronted Me in the day of My calamity, but The Lord was My Support. 18 The Lord rewarded Me according to My Righteousness; according to The Cleanness Of My Hands He Has Recompensed Me. 20

For I have kept The Ways of the Lord, and have not wickedly departed from My God. 21 For all His Judgments were before Me, and I did not put away His Statutes from Me. 22 I was also blameless before Him, and I kept Myself from My iniquity. 23 Therefore the Lord has recompensed Me according to My Righteousness, according to The Cleanness of My Hands in His Sight. 24

With The Merciful You will show Yourself Merciful; with a blameless man, You will show Yourself Blameless; 25 With the pure You will show Yourself Pure; and with the devious You will show Yourself shrewd. 26 For You will save the humble people, but will bring down the haughty looks. 27 For You will light My Lamp; The Lord My God will Enlighten my darkness. 28 For by You I can run against a troop, by My God I can leap over a wall. 29

As for God, His Way Is Perfect; the Word of the Lord Is Proven; He is A Shield to all who trust In Him. 30 For who is God, except The Lord? And who is A Rock, except Our God? 31 It is God who arms Me with strength, and makes My way perfect. 32 He make my feet like the feet of the deer, and set Me on My High Places. 33 He teaches My Hands to make war, so that My Arms can bend a bow of bronze. 34

You have also given Me the Shield of Your Salvation; Your Right Hand has held Me up. Your Gentleness has made Me great. 35 You enlarged My Path under Me, so My Feet did not slip. 36 I have pursued my enemies and overtaken them; neither did I turn back again until they were destroyed. 37 I have wounded them, so that they could not rise; they have fallen under My Feet. 38

For You have armed Me with strength for the battle; You have subdues under Me those who rose up against Me. 39 You have also given Me the necks of My enemies, so that I destroyed those who hated Me. 40 They cried out, but there was none to save; even To The Lord, but He did not answer them. 41 Then I beat them as fine as the dust before the wind; I cast them out like dirt in the streets. 42

You have delivered Me from the strivings of the people; You have made Me the head of the nation; a people I have not known shall serve Me. 43 As soon as They Hear Of Me they Obey Me; the foreigners submit to Me. 44 The foreigner fade away, and come frightened from their hideouts. 45

The Lord Lives! Blessed be My Rock! Let The God Of My Salvation Be Exalted. 46 It is God who avenges Me, and subdues the people under Me; 47 He Delivers Me from My enemies, You also lift me up above those who rise against Me; You have Delivered Me from the violent man. 48 Therefore I will give thanks To You, O Lord, among the Gentiles, and sing praises to Your Name. 49 Great Deliverance He gives to His King, and shows Mercy to His Anointed, to David and His descendants forevermore. 50

Who is like a wise man? And who knows the interpretation of a thing? A man's wisdom makes his face shine, and the sternness of his face is changed. Ecclesiastes 8:1 I say, "Keep the King's Commandment for The Sake to Your Oath to God. 2 Do not be hasty to go out from His Presence. Do not take your stand for as evil thing, for He does whatever Pleases Him." 3

There is an evil I have seen under the sun, as an error proceeding from the ruler: 10:5 Folly is set in great dignity, while the rich sit in a lowly place. 6 I have seen servants on horses, while princes walk on the ground like servants. 7

"Say Now to the rebellious house: 'Do you no know these things mean?' Tell them, 'Indeed the king of Babylon went to Jerusalem and took its king and princes, and led them with him to Babylon. Ezekiel 17:12 You have indeed been trapped, O Babylon, and you were not aware; you have been found and also caught, because you have contended against The Lord. Jeremiah 50:24 The Voice of those who flee and escape from the land of Babylon 'Declares In Zion' The Vengeance Of The Lord Our God, The Vengeance Of His Temple." 28

"Call together the archers against Babylon. All you who bend the bow encamp against it all around; let none of them escape. Repay her according to her work; according to all she has done, do to her; for she has been proud against The Lord, against The Holy One of Israel. 29 Therefore her young men shall fall in the streets, and all her men of war shall be cut off in That Day. 30 The most proud shall stumble and fall and no one will rise up; I will kindle a fire in his cities, and it will devour all around." 32

"And I will repay Babylon and all the inhabitants of Chaldea for all the evil they have done in Zion in your sight," says The Lord, 51:24 "Behold, I AM against you, O destroying mountain, who destroys all the earth," says The Lord. "And I will stretch out My Hand against you, roll you down from the rocks, and make you a burnt mountain. 25 They shall not take from you a stone for a corner nor a stone for a foundation, but you shall be desolate forever," says The Lord. 26

"And the land will tremble and sorrow; for Every Purpose of the Lord Shall Be Performed against Babylon, to make the land of Babylon a desolation without inhabitant. 29 Let the violence done to Me and My flesh be upon Babylon, the inhabitant of Zion will say; and My blood be upon the inhabitants of Chaldea!" Jerusalem will say. 35

I will punish Baal in Babylon, and I will bring out of his mouth what he has swallowed; and the nations shall not stream to him anymore. Yes the wall of Babylon shall fall. 44 My People, go out of the midst of her! And let everyone deliver himself from The Fierce Anger of the Lord. 45

And I heard another Voice from heaven saying, "Come out of her, My People, lest you share in her sins, and lest you receive of her plaques. Revelation 18:4 For her sins have reached to heaven, and God has remembered her iniquities. 5 Therefore her plaques will come in One Day---- death and mourning and famine. And she will be utterly burned with fire, for strong is The Lord God who judges her." 8

"Rejoice over her, O heaven, and you Holy Apostles and Prophets, For God has avenged you on her!" 20 Then a mighty angel took up a stone like a great millstone and threw it into the sea, saying, 'Thus with violence the great city Babylon shall be thrown down, and shall not be found anymore." 21

"The sound of harpists, musicians, flutists, and trumpeters shall not be heard in you anymore. No craftsman of any craft shall be found in you anymore, and the sound of millstone shall not be heard in you anymore. 22 The light of a lamp shall not shine in you anymore, and The Voice of the Bridegroom and Bride shall not be heard in you anymore. For your merchants were the great men of the earth, for by your sorcery all the nations were deceived. 23 And in her was found the blood of the prophets and saints, and of all who were slain on the earth." 24

"Look among the nations and watch---- be utterly astounded! For I will work A Work in Your Days which you would not believe, though it were told you. Habakkuk 1:5 For indeed I AM raising up the Chaldeans, a bitter and hasty nation which marches through the breadth of the earth, to possess dwelling places that are not theirs. 6 They are terrible and dreadful; their judgment and their dignity proceed from themselves." 7

"They all come for violence; their faces are set like the east wind. They gather captives like sand. 9 They scoff at kings, and princes are scorned by them. They deride every stronghold, for they heap up earthen mounds and seize it. 10 Shall they therefore empty their net, and continue to slay the nations without pity? "17

Then The Lord answered Me and said: "Write the Vision and make it plain in tablets that he may run who reads It. 2:2

Woe to him who builds a town with bloodshed, who establishes a city by iniquity! 12 Behold, is it not of The Lord of Hosts that the peoples labor to feed the fire, and the nations weary themselves in vain? 13 For the earth will be filled with The Knowledge of the Glory of the Lord, as the waters cover the sea. 14

There shall Come Forth a Rod from The Stem of Jesse, and A Branch shall grow out of his roots. Isaiah 11:1 The Spirit of the Lord shall rest upon Him, The Spirit of Wisdom and Understanding, The Spirit of Counsel and Might, The Spirit of Knowledge and of The Fear of the Lord. 2 His delight is in The Fear Of The Lord, and He shall not judge by the sight of His eyes, nor decide by the hearing of the ears; 3 But With Righteousness He shall judge the poor, and decide with equity for the meek of the earth; He shall strike the earth with the rod of His Mouth, and with the breath of His Lips He shall slay the wicked. 4

"And In That Day there shall be A Root of Jesse, who shall stand As a Banner to the people; for the Gentiles shall seek Him, and His Resting Place shall Be Glorious. 10 It shall come to pass In That Day that The Lord shall set His Hand again The Second Time to Recover The Remnant of His People who are left, from Assyria and Egypt, from Pathros and Cush, from Elam and Shinar, from Hamath and the island of the sea." 11

He will set A Banner for the nations, and will assemble the outcasts of Israel, and Gather Together the dispersed of Judah from The Four Corners of the Earth. 12 And In That Day you will say: "O Lord, I will Praise You; though You were angry with me, Your anger is turned away, and You Comfort Me. 12:1 Behold, God Is My Salvation, I will trust and not be afraid; 'For YAH,

The Lord, is My Strength and Song; He also has become My Salvation.'" 2

Therefore, with joy you will draw water from The Wells of Salvation. 3 And In That Day, you will say: "Praise the Lord, Call upon His Name; Declare His Deeds among the peoples, make mention that His Name Is Exalted. 4 Sing to The Lord, for He has done excellent things; this is known in all the earth. 5 Cry out and Shout, O Inhabitants of Zion, for Great Is the Holy One of Israel in your midst!" 6

"Lift up A Banner on the high mountain, Raise Your Voice to them; wave your hand that they may enter The Gates of the Nobles. 13:2 I have commanded My Sanctified Ones, I have also Called My Mighty Ones for My Anger----Those Who Rejoice in My Exaltation." 3

The noise of a multitude in the mountains, like that of many people! A tumultuous noise of the kingdoms of nations Gathered Together! The Lord of Hosts musters The Army for battle. 4 They come from a far country, from the end of heaven---- The Lord and His Weapons of Indignation, to destroy the whole land. 5

Behold, The Day of the Lord Comes, cruel, with both wrath and fierce anger, to lay the land desolate; and He will destroy the sinners from it. 9 For the stars of heaven and their constellations will not give their light; the sun will be darkened in its going forth, and the moon will not cause its light to shine. 10

"I will punish the world for its evil, and the wicked for their iniquity; I will halt the arrogance of the proud and lay low the haughtiness of the terrible. 11 I will make a mortal rarer than fine gold, a man more than the golden wedge of Ophir. 12 And Babylon, the glory of kingdoms, the beauty of the Chaldeans' pride, will be as when God overthrew Sodom and Gomorrah." 19

You are wearied in the length of your way; yet you did not say, 'There is no hope.' You have found the life of your hand; therefore you were not grieved. 57:10 "And of whom have you been afraid, or feared, that you have lied and not remembered Me, nor taken it to your heart? Is it not because I have held My Peace from of old that you do not Fear Me?" 11

"I will declare your righteousness and your works, for they will not profit you. 12 When you cry out, let your collection of idols deliver you. But the wind will carry them all away, A Breath will take them. But he who puts his Trust in Me shall possess the land, and shall inherit My Holy Mountain." 13

And One shall say, "Heap it up! Heap it Up! Prepare the Way, take the stumbling block out of The Way of My People." 14 For Thus says The High and Lofty One Who Inhabits Eternity, Whose Name Is Holy: "I dwell in The High and Holy Place, with him who has a contrite and humble spirit, To Revive the Spirit of the humble, and To Revive the Heart of The Contrite Ones." 15

Sing aloud to God our strength; make a joyful shout to The God of Jacob. Psalms 81:1 Raise a song and strike the timbrel, the pleasant harp with the lute. 2 Blow the trumpet at the time of the new moon, at the full moon, on our solemn feast day. 3 For this is a statute for Israel, A Law of The God of Jacob. 4

This He established in Joseph as A Testimony, when He went throughout the land of Egypt, where I heard a language I did not understand. 5 "I removed his shoulder from the burden; his hands were freed from the baskets. 6 You called in trouble, and I delivered you; I answered you in The Secret Place of thunder; I tested you at The Waters of Meribah." Selah 7

"Hear, O My People, and I will admonish you! O Israel, if you will Listen to Me! 8 There shall be no foreign god among you; nor shall you worship any foreign god. 9 I AM The Lord Your God, who brought you out of the land of Egypt; open your mouth wide, and I will fill it." 10

"But My People would not heed My Voice, and Israel would have none of Me. 11 So I gave them up to their own stubborn heart, to walk in their own counsels. 12 Oh that My People would Listen to Me that Israel would Walk in My Ways! 13 I would soon subdue their enemies, and turn My Hand against their adversaries. 14 The haters of The Lord would pretend submission to Him, but their fate would endure forever. 15 He would have fed them also with the finest of wheat; and with honey from the rock I would have satisfied you." 16

"I will stretch out My Hand against Judah, and against all the inhabitants of Jerusalem. I will cut off every trace of Baal from this place, the names of the idolatrous priests with the pagan priests---- Zephaniah 1:4 Those who worship the hosts of heaven on the housetops; those who worship and swear oaths by The Lord, but who also swear by MILCOM; 5 Those who turn back from following The Lord, and have not sought The Lord." 6

Be silent in The Presence Of The Lord God; for The Day of The Lord Is At Hand, for The Lord has prepared a sacrifice; He has invited His Guests. 7 "And it shall be In The Day Of The Lord's Sacrifice, that I will punish the princes and the king's children, and such as are clothed with foreign apparel. 8 In the same day I will punish all those who leap over the threshold, who fill their masters' houses with violence and deceit." 9

"And it shall come to pass at That Time that I will search Jerusalem with lamps, and punish the men who are settled in complacency, who say in their heart, 'The Lord will not do good, nor will He do evil.' 12 Therefore their goods shall become booty, and their houses a desolation; they shall build houses, but not inhabit them; they shall plant vineyards, but not drink their wine." 13

The Great Day of the Lord is near; it is near and hastens quickly. The noise of The Day of the Lord is bitter; there the mighty men shall cry out. 14 That Day is a day of wrath, a day of trouble and distress, a day of devastation and desolation, a day of darkness and gloominess, a day of clouds and thick darkness, 15 A Day Of Trumpet and alarm against the fortified cities and against the high towers. 16

"I will bring distress upon men, and they shall walk like blind men, because they have sinned against The Lord; their blood shall be poured out like dust, and their flesh like refuse." 17 Neither their silver nor their gold shall be able to deliver them In The Day Of The Lord's Wrath; but the whole land shall be devoured By The Fire Of His Jealousy, for He will make speedy riddance of all those who dwell in the land. 18

Woe to the inhabitants of the seacoast, the nation of the Cherethites! The Word of the Lord is against you, O Canaan, land of the Philistines: I will destroy you; so there shall be no inhabitant. 2:5 The seacoast shall be pastures, with shelters for shepherds and folds for flocks. 6 The coast shall be for The Remnant of Judah; they shall feed their flocks there, in the house of Ashkelon they shall lie down at evening. For The Lord their God will intervene for them, and return their captives. 7

"I have heard the reproach of Moab, and the insults of the people of Ammon, with which they have reproached My People, and made arrogant threats against their borders. 8 Therefore, as I Live," says The Lord of Hosts, The God of Israel, "Surely Moab shall be like Sodom, and the people of Ammon like Gomorrah----overrun with weeds and salt pits, and a perpetual desolation. The residue of My People shall plunder them, and The Remnant of My People shall possess them."

This they shall have for their pride, because they have reproached and made arrogant threats against The People of The Lord of Hosts. 10 The Lord will be awesome to them, for He will reduce to nothing all the gods of the earth; people shall Worship Him, each one from his place, indeed all the shores of the nations. 11

"Therefore wait for Me," says The Lord, "Until the Day I Rise up for plunder; My Determination is To Gather the nation to My Assembly of Kingdoms, to pour on the My Indignation, all My fierce anger; all the earth shall be devoured with the fire of My Jealousy. 3:8 For then I WILL RESTORE to the peoples A Pure Language, that they all may Call on The Name Of The Lord, to serve him with One Accord." 9

In That Day, you shall not be shamed for any of your deeds in which you transgress against Me; for then I will take away from your midst those who rejoice in your pride, and you shall no longer be haughty In My Holy Mountain. 11 I will leave in your midst a meek and humble people, and they shall Trust In The Name Of the Lord. 12 The Remnant of Israel shall do no unrighteousness and speak no lies, nor shall a deceitful tongue be found in their mouth; for they shall feed their flock and lie down, and no one shall make them afraid.

In That Day, it shall be said to Jerusalem: "Do not fear; Zion, let not your hands be weak. 16 The Lord Your God in Your Midst, The Mighty One, will Save; He will rejoice over you with gladness, He will quiet you with His Love, He will rejoice over you with singing. 17

"I will gather those who sorrow over The Appointed Assembly, who are among you, to whom its reproach is a burden. 18 Behold, at That Time I will deal with all who afflict you; I will save the lame, and gather those who were driven out; I will appoint them for praise and fame in every land where they were put to shame. 19 At That Time I will bring you back, even at The Time I

Gather You; for I will give you fame and praise among all the peoples of the earth, when I return your captives before your eyes," says The Lord. 20

Now therefore, thus says The Lord of Hosts: "Consider your ways!" Haggai 1:5 "You have sown much, and bring in little; you eat, but do not have enough; you drink, but you are not filled with drink; you clothe yourselves, but no one is warm; and he who earns wages, earns wages to put into a sack with holes." 6

"You looked for much, but indeed it came too little; and when you brought it home, I blew it away. Why?" says The Lord of Hosts. "Because of My House that is in ruins, while every one of you runs to his own house. 9 'Who is left among you who saw This Temple in Its Former Glory? And how do you see it now? In comparison with it, is this not in your eyes as nothing?'" 2:3

"For thus says The Lord Of Hosts: 'Once more {it is A Little While} I will shake the heaven and earth, the sea and dry land; 6 'And I will shake the nations, and they shall Come to The Desire Of All Nations, and I will fill This Temple with Glory,' says The Lord Of Hosts. 7 The Glory of This Latter Temple shall be greater than the former,' says The Lord of Hosts. 'And In This Place I Will Give Peace,' says The Lord of Hosts." 9

"Sing and Rejoice, O Daughter Of Zion! For Behold, I AM COMING and I will dwell in your midst," says The Lord. Zechariah 2:10 "Many nations shall be joined to The Lord in That Day, and they shall become My People. And I will dwell in their midst. Then you Will Know that The Lord of Hosts has Sent Me to You. 11 And the

Lord will take possession of Judah as His Inheritance in the Holy Land, and will again choose Jerusalem. 12 Be Silent, all flesh, before The Lord, for He is aroused from His Holy Habitation!" 13

And The Lord said to Satan, "The Lord rebuke you, Satan! The Lord who has chosen Jerusalem rebuke you! Is this not A Brand plucked from The Fire? 3:2 'When you eat and when you drink, do you not eat and drink for yourselves? 7:6 Should you not have Obeyed The Words Which The Lord Proclaimed through the former prophets when Jerusalem and the cities around it were inhabited and prosperous, and the south and the lowland were inhabited?'" 7

"Thus says The Lord of Hosts: 'Execute TRUE JUSTICE, show mercy and compassion everyone to his neighbor. 9 Do not oppress the widow of the fatherless, the alien or the poor. Let none of you plan evil in his heart against his brother.' 10 But they refused To Heed, shrugged their shoulders, and stopped their ears so that they could not hear. 11 Yes, they made their heart like flint, refusing to hear The Law and The Words, which The Lord of Hosts had sent By His Spirit through the former prophets. Thus great wrath came from The Lord of Hosts." 12

Thus says The Lord of Hosts: "I AM zealous for Zion with great zeal; with great fervor I AM zealous for Her." 8:2 "Thus says The Lord: 'I will Return to Zion, and dwell in the midst of Jerusalem. Jerusalem shall be called The City of Truth, The Mountain of The Lord Of Hosts, and The Holy Mountain.'" 3

"Thus says The Lord of Hosts: 'Old men and old women shall again sit in the streets of Jerusalem, each one with his staff in his hand because of great age. 4 The streets of the city shall be full of boys and girls playing in its streets.' 5 "Thus says The Lord of Hosts: 'If it is marvelous in the eyes of The Remnant of this people In These Days, will it also be marvelous In My Eyes?' says The Lord of Hosts." 6

"Thus says The Lord of Hosts: 'People shall yet Come, inhabitants of many cities; the inhabitants of one city shall go to another, saying, "Let us continue to go and pray Before the Lord, and Seek the Lord of Hosts. I Myself Will Go Also." 21 Yes many people and strong nations shall Come to Seek the Lord of Hosts in Jerusalem, and to pray before The Lord.' 22 "Thus says The Lord Of Hosts: 'In Those Days ten men from every language of the nations shall grasp The Sleeve of A Jewish Man, saying, "Let us go with You, for we have heard That God Is With You."'" 23

I Will Whistle for them and Gather them, for I Will Redeem Them; and they shall increase as they once increased. 10:8 "I will show them among the peoples, and they Shall Remember Me in far countries; they shall live, together with their children, and they Shall Return. 9 I will also bring them back from the land of Egypt, and gather them from Assyria. I will bring them into the land of Gilead and Lebanon, until no more room is found for them." 10

"And it shall happen In That Day that I will make Jerusalem a very heavy stone for all peoples; all who would heave it away will surely be cut in pieces, though all nations of the earth are gathered against it. 12:3 It shall be In That Day that I will seek to destroy all the nations that come against Jerusalem." 9

"In That Day a fountain shall be opened for The House of David and for the inhabitants of Jerusalem, for sin and uncleanness. 13:1 'It shall be In That Day,' says The Lord of Hosts, 'that I will cut off the name of the idols from the land, and they shall no more be remembered. I will also cause the prophets and unclean spirit to depart from the land.'" 2

And In That Day His Feet will stand on The Mount Of Olives, which faces Jerusalem on the east. And The Mount Of Olives shall be split in two, from east to west, making a very large valley; half of the mountain shall move toward the north and half of it toward the south. 14:4 Then you shall flee through My mountain valley, for the mountain valley shall reach to Azal, Yes, you shall flee as you fled from the earthquake in the days of Uzziah king of Judah. Thus the Lord My God will come, and all The Saints with You. 5

It shall come to pass In That Day that there will be no light; the lights will be diminish. It shall be one day, which Is Known to the Lord---- neither day nor night, But at evening time it shall happen that t will be light. 7 And In That Day, it shall be That Living Waters shall flow from Jerusalem, half of them toward The Eastern Sea and half of them toward The Western Sea; in both summer and winter, it shall occur. 8 And the Lord shall

be King over all the earth. In That Day it shall be----
"The Lord Is One," and His Name One. 9

And this shall be The Plague with which The Lord
will strike all the people who fought against Jerusalem:
their flesh shall dissolve while they stand on their feet,
their eyes shall dissolve in their sockets, and their
tongue shall dissolve in their mouths. 12

"Thus says The Lord God: 'This is Jerusalem; I have
set her in the midst of the nations and the countries
all around her. Ezekiel 5:5 She has rebelled against My
Judgments by doing wickedness more than the nations,
and against My Statutes more than the countries that
are all around her; for they have refused My Judgments,
and they have not walked in My Statutes.'" 6

"Therefore thus says The Lord God: 'Because you
have multiplied disobedience more than the nations
that are all around you, have not walked in My Statutes
nor kept My Judgments, nor even done according to the
judgments of the nations that are all around you--- 7
Therefore thus says The Lord God: Indeed I, even I, am
against you and will execute judgments in your midst in
the sight of the nations. 8 And I will do among you what
I have never done, and the like of which I Will never do
again, because of all your abominations." 9

"Son of Man, set Your Face toward the mountains
of Israel, and prophesy against them, 6:2 And say, 'O
mountains of Israel, Hear the Word of the Lord God!
Thus says The Lord God to the mountains, to the hills,
to the ravines, and to the valleys: "Indeed I, even I,
will bring a sword against you, and I will destroy your

high places, 3 Then your altars shall be desolate, your incense altars shall be broken, and I will cast down your slain men before your idols." 4

"And I will lay the corpses of The Children of Israel before their idols, and I will scatter your bones all around your altars. 5 In all your dwelling places the cities shall be laid waste, and the high places shall be desolate, so that your altars may be laid waste and made desolate, your idols made be broken and made to cease, your incense altars may be cut down, and your works may be abolished. 6 The slain shall fall in your midst, and you shall know that I AM The Lord." 7

"Yet I will leave A Remnant, so that you have some who escape the sword among the nations, when you are scattered through the countries. 8 Then those of you who escape will Remember Me among the nations where they are carried away captive, because I was crushed by their adulterous heart which as departed from Me, and by their eyes which played the harlot after their idols; they will loathe themselves for the evils which they committed in all their abominations. 9 And they shall know that I AM The Lord; I have not said in vain that I would bring this calamity upon them." 10

Hear The Word of the Lord, you children of Israel, for The Lord brings a charge against the inhabitants of the land: "There is no Truth or Mercy or Knowledge of God in the land. Hosea 4:1 By swearing and lying, killing and stealing and committing adultery, they break all restraint, with bloodshed upon bloodshed. 2 Now let no man contend, or rebuke another; for your people are like those who contend with the priest." 4

My People are destroyed For Lack Of Knowledge. Because you have Rejected Knowledge, I also reject you from being priest for Me; because you have forgotten The Law of Your God, I also will forget your children. 6 The more they increased, the more they sinned against Me; I will change their glory into shame. 7

The pride of Israel testifies to his face; therefore, Israel and Ephraim stumble in their iniquity; Judah also stumbles with them. 5:5 "With their flocks and herds they shall go To Seek the Lord, but they will not find Him; He has withdrawn Himself from them. 6 They have dealt treacherously with The Lord, for they have begotten pagan children. Now a New Moon shall devour them and their heritage." 7

Come, and let us Return To the Lord; for He has torn, but He will heal us; He has stricken, but He will bind us up. 6:1 After two days He will Revive Us; on The Third Day He will raise us up, that we may live with Him In His Sight. 2 Let us know, let us pursue The Knowledge of the Lord. His going forth is established as the morning; He will come to us like the rain, like the latter and former rain to the earth. 3

Therefore, I have hewn them by The Prophets, I have slain them by The Words of My Mouth; and your judgments are like light that goes forth. 5 For I desire mercy and not sacrifice, and The Knowledge of God more than burnt offerings. 6 "But like men they transgressed The Covenant; there they dealt treacherously with Me. 7

They do not consider in their hearts that I remember all their wickedness; nor their own deeds surrounded them; they are before My Face. 7:2 they make a king glad with their wickedness, and the princes with their lies. 3 "They are all adulterers. Like an oven heater by a baker----, he ceases stirring the fire after kneading the dough, until it is leavened. 4

"Not everyone who says to Me, 'Lord, Lord.' shall enter The Kingdom of Heaven, but he who does The Will of the Father in heaven Matthew 7:21 Many will say to Me In That Day, 'Lord, Lord, have we not prophesied In You Name, cast out demons In Your Name, and done many wonders In Your Name?' 22 And then I will declare to them. 'I never knew you; depart from Me, you who practice lawlessness!'" 23

"Therefore whoever hears these sayings of Mine, and does them, I will liken him to a wise man who built his house on the rock: 24 And the rain descended. The floods came, and the winds blew and beat on the house and it did not fall, for it was founded on the rock." 25

"But everyone who hears these sayings of Mine, and does not do them, will be like a foolish man who built his house on the sand: 26 and the rain descended, the floods came, and the wind blew and beat on that house; and it fell. And great was its fall." 27

And so it was, when Jesus had ended these sayings, that the people were astonished at His Teaching, 28 For He taught them as One Having Authority, and not as the scribes. 29 "Come To Me, all you who labor and are heavy laden, and I Will Give You Rest. 11:28 Take My yoke upon you and learn from Me, for I AM gentle and lowly in heart, and you will find rest for your souls. 29 For My yoke is easy and My burden is light." 30

Then the Pharisees went out and plotted against Him, how they might destroy Him. 12:14 But when Jesus knew it, He withdrew from there. And great multitudes followed Him, and He healed them all. 15 Yet He warned them not to make Him Known, 16 That it might be fulfilled which was spoken By Isaiah The Prophet, saying: "Behold! My Servant Whom I Have Chosen, My Beloved in Whom My Soul Is Well Pleased! I Will Put My Spirit Upon Him, And He Will Declare Justice To The Gentiles." 18

For there is no partiality with God. Romans 2:11 For as many as have sinned without law will also perish without law, and as many as have sinned in The Law will be judged By The Law, 12 (For not the hearers of The Law are just in The Sight Of God, but The Doers Of The Law Will Be Justified,) 13

As it is written: "There is none righteous, no, not one; 3:10 There is none who understands; there is none who Seeks After God. 11 They have all turned aside; they have together become unprofitable; there is none who does good, no, not one." 12

Jesus said to them, "Have you never read in The Scriptures: 'The Stone which the builders rejected has become The Chief Cornerstone. This was The Lord's Doing, and it is marvelous In Our Eyes'? Matthew 21:42 Therefore I say to you, The Kingdom of God will be taken from you and given to a nation bearing fruits of it. 43 For many are called, but few are Chosen." 22:14

Milton Keynes UK
Ingram Content Group UK Ltd.
UKHW030909271124
451618UK00013B/355/J

9 798369 433577